HOODOO

A LITTLE INTRODUCTION

Donyae Coles

Illustrated by
Sabrena Khadija

RP MINIS

PHILADELPHIA

RP Minis®
Hachette Book Group
1290 Avenue of the Americas, New York, NY 10104
www.runningpress.com
@Running_Press

First Edition: August 2024

Published by RP Minis, an imprint of Hachette Book Group, Inc. The RP Minis name and logo is a registered trademark of Hachette Book Group, Inc.

Running Press books may be purchased in bulk for business, educational, or promotional use. For more information, please contact your local bookseller or the Hachette Book Group Special Markets Department at Special.Markets@hbgusa.com.

The publisher is not responsible for websites (or their content) that are not owned by the publisher.

Text by Donyae Coles
Design by Amanda Richmond

Library of Congress Control Number: 2023951464

ISBN: 978-0-7624-8594-9 (hardcover)

Printed in China

HH

10 9 8 7 6 5 4 3 2 1

CONTENTS

7
WHAT IS HOODOO?

29
ANCESTOR VENERATION

47
ALTARS

69
WHAT DO YOU NEED
FOR HOODOO?

85

DIVINATION

103

THE WORK

143

PARTING WORDS

WHAT IS HOODOO?

⊙ ∘∘∘ ⊙

SWEET-AND-SOUR JARS, HOT footin', uncrossing candles, and dressing oils are all fairly common practices in magical or spiritual communities. You can find supplies for many of these rituals at any occult shop. These practices and rituals have become so ubiquitous that now they seem like just a general part of magical practices. But they're not.

All these things—and more—come from Hoodoo.

Most people have heard the term *Hoodoo* at least in passing. Even among those who don't have any interest in spirituality, it's often found mentioned in books, movies, comics, and so on. Despite that exposure, though, many still don't know what Hoodoo is.

Hoodoo goes by a variety of names. It is also known as *conjure* and *rootwork*, the latter for an obvious reason! The practice relies heavily on plants, herbs, and roots. Hoodoo is a form of sympathetic magic, which means it's based around the concept of "like attracts like." There is also a good deal of what is commonly thought of as "superstition" in Hoodoo. The practice itself is not just a performance of spells—also called *work*—but is instead a way of looking at and interacting with the world. Veneration of ancestors and respect for natural spirits are core aspects of the practice that reinforce our connections with all that we come into contact with.

Hoodoo is a rich cultural practice that comes from African American folk magic.

It is based in principles of protection, healing, and community. Although Hoodoo is often inaccurately depicted as being about work that causes harm, such as curses, that is in opposition to what the practice is for. While it is true that various aggressive works can be done, those are not the majority of spells and rituals performed by rootworkers and followers.

Hoodoo was created by enslaved Africans to help heal and protect them. It incorporates a number of African beliefs, as well as Indigenous North American and European ones. The practice of Hoodoo began on plantations in the antebellum

South and grew and evolved
as the needs of Black people
changed over the decades. As
formerly enslaved Black people
began to migrate to other parts
of the United States, Hoodoo
formed distinct branches based
around the needs of the people
as well as the availability of
the natural materials in those
regions. It continues to be

practiced to this day, both publicly and privately.

Within the work of Hoodoo, there are all types of rituals for anything from gaining money

 to protecting one's home, finding love, and increasing your luck. In fact, for pretty much any

problem in daily life, there is
a Hoodoo practice meant to
help solve it. There is no issue
too small or too large to be
addressed with Hoodoo.

Hoodoo was created as
a practical solution for the
problems that the people who
practiced it were facing. The
need for money, protection of
the home from aggression, and

keeping the family together and healthy are just a few of the very real, very common needs of Black people during the time of Hoodoo's creation. This is also why the tools and supplies needed for the practice are so simple and common—so they can be sourced by people who have very few means.

Hoodoo is not just peaceful work. There are also rituals, powders, and work meant to harm or overpower others. Many spiritual people have decried these works, but this is the wrong way of thinking about them. The context in which Hoodoo came to be calls for the existence of such practices, and it is not wrong to utilize them. Love, revenge, and banishment all have their place and can be used responsibly to protect people.

WHAT
HOODOO IS NOT

Hoodoo is often mistaken for
Voodoo (Voudon), Santeria,
and a number of other African
traditional religions (ATRs)
that are still practiced in Africa
as well as throughout the
diaspora. Although Hoodoo
may share commonalities with

those practices, they are all distinct, separate traditions with their own beliefs.

Though it is a stand-alone system, Hoodoo is often practiced in conjunction with other religions. The most familiar and well-known of these blends is the use of Christian beliefs and prayers, most notably the use of psalms, in many works. This is due to the long-standing connection of many African Americans to Christianity in the United States. It is not necessary, however, to blend Hoodoo with aspects of a Christian faith. People who are interested in practicing do not need to involve Christianity or any other religious practice to work with Hoodoo.

You can practice Hoodoo without other beliefs—many people do! For those who do wish to combine Hoodoo with a religious practice, the most common is Christianity, but many African Americans also practice Hoodoo in conjunction with other ATRs.

WHAT IS HOODOO FOR?

Hoodoo can be used to aid in anything you struggle with or to draw in what you want to bring into your everyday life. There are love-focused acts to find a new partner or hold on to your current one, and there are works for revenge or

malice. But these two ends of
the spectrum are not the only
things this rich practice has to
offer. There's literally a work
for anything and everything!

If you're looking for a new

job or apartment,
there is work to
be done there.
If you're having
a streak of bad

luck or just going to the casino with your friends, there are all kinds of practices that bring you luck. But remember, Hoodoo was a practice created to heal and protect, so there are many, many works focused on protecting the self, home, and family from a wide variety of dangers.

ANCESTOR VENERATION

❖ ⊹ ⊹ ❖

THE PRACTICE OF HONORING
one's ancestors is an
important part of Hoodoo.
Many people don't understand
this tradition and believe
people who practice Hoodoo

"worship" their ancestors like one would worship a god, but that is not the case!

Veneration means to honor, to give respect to. The venerating of ancestors is done to celebrate and remember those who came before us, as their spirits will guide and help their living descendants on their own journeys through life. This is separate from any beliefs that the practitioner may have in any gods, spirits, or "higher powers."

Honoring ancestors can be done in many ways, from hanging their photos in your home and speaking to them to setting a plate of their favorite foods on your altar for them. For some people, it

is just telling their stories and
remembering them.

WHO IS AN ANCESTOR?

Ancestors are those who came before us. They are members of our families and our communities who were part of our lives and the lives of the people close to us and who have passed on—but their power and care remain. The line of ancestors extends from you all the way back, further than anyone can remember. A person cannot know all their ancestors, but that is alright; they know you. To be clear, an ancestor is anyone who has passed on who you have connection with whether known or unknown to you.

Some people have trouble

with this because, for a
variety of reasons, they may
not know their family. They
may be estranged or adopted
and believe that they cannot
connect with their ancestors as
a result. Their closest relatives
may have caused them great
harm before passing, and they
believe they have no ancestors
to call on.

But ancestors are *everyone* who has come before. Even if you do not know them by name or face. It is *everyone* who is connected to you by blood or community.

Making offerings to ancestors is a good way to increase your comfort in working with them. Offerings fall into the following three broad categories:

▶ **Food–**This could be a small plate of your own dinner or a loved one's favorite food. Fruits, vegetables, meats, cakes, food! It is given at regular intervals and set on your altar or other sacred space. How long you leave it out will depend on your circumstances. You may only be able to let it sit for the space of the meal or

overnight. Do not wait for it
to become a biohazard before
you clean it up. If your space
is outside, you may leave the
offering for as long as you
like. Ideally what is left would
be buried or composted to
return it to the earth, but don't
feel bad about dropping it in
the trash.

▶ **Drink**—Much like food, this could be a preferred drink of an ancestor you knew—for example, if your grandmother had a fondness for bug juice or lemonade, you can leave that. If you do not know what they would like, the common go-to is alcohol, such as gin or whiskey. Pour a small amount into a cup or glass and set it out, like the food. You can let this evaporate or clean it up after the space of a meal has passed.

▶ **Money–**Most people like money, and the way to offer it is to burn it, which might sound frightening for those not familiar with Hoodoo. But don't worry. This is where Hoodoo's status as a sympathetic practice comes in handy, because it isn't necessary to use real legal tender. Many people use hell money instead, a Chinese product that is commonly sold in occult shops. Hell money refers to bills created to offer to the dead. You can also use images of money or write checks if you have them. Burn this before your ancestor image or idol.

It may feel uncomfortable at first to engage with ancestors in this way, especially if this is the first time that you've done something like this. That's alright! Pay attention

to those feelings, as they
may be guidance to change
something about your process.
Try many things until you are
comfortable.

A NOTE
ON RESPECT

Ancestors, all of them, were once living people and should be treated respectfully. They are not servants or impersonal spirits called upon for favors. When working with the ancestors, you should approach them as you would

want to be approached and
spoken to when you are one
day an ancestor.

ALTARS

AN IMPORTANT PART OF THE practice is having a space for working, leaving offerings, and so on. This is the altar space. Often, when we think of altars, we think of very formal spaces, but yours doesn't have to be. An altar space can be as simple as a table with your grandparents' photographs on it and a spot to light a candle. In fact, many African American homes have unofficial altar spaces set up without their inhabitants realizing it. Walls adorned with the photos of family that have passed, tables set with only the Bible and a candle, and the like are all examples of altar spaces!

Creating an altar space is a personal practice and is based on the needs of the person creating it. It does not have to be large, and it does not have to encompass the entirety of your practice. It should be a space that feels safe and accessible to you.

Space to leave offerings is also important to have on

your altar. In Hoodoo, the altar space is a working, living space. Even if you are planning to work in a larger area, it is important to have an area on your altar where you can make offerings to your ancestors or whomever else you may feel inclined to pay tribute.

Your altar should be a sacred space for you and should

reflect the things you find
sacred. Some may want to
draw on the natural world,
with crystals, found feathers,
flowers, and other items
from nature.

Someone who
is more drawn
to ritualistic
space may have
idols depicting

gods and sacred objects. It is
really up to the person who is
using the space to determine
what speaks to them. Even
so, there are two categories of
altars we will discuss here, the
permanent and the moveable.

PERMANENT ALTAR SPACES

A permanent altar space is a stable fixture in your home. It does not have to be large, but it may include items that are not easily moved. It is usually located in a section of the home that is accessible and comfortable. It can be in your

kitchen, living room, or even in
a closet if you would prefer to
be able to close it off for privacy.
The space should be outside of
a high-traffic area so that works
are not disturbed by the comings
and goings of the household.

➤ **surface**–A space for placing objects and doing work. This can be a small table or even a bookcase. The surface should be flat so nothing falls over.

▶ **Covering**—Your surface should be covered before anything is placed upon it. This is usually done with a plain white or black cloth, but you can use any cloth that holds meaning to you. The important thing is that the surface is covered.

➤ **A working area**–On top
of the cloth there should be
an easy-to-clean, fireproof
workspace. Hoodoo practice
involves a lot of different,
sometimes messy, components.
But even just spilling some
water can cause a huge mess, so
it's better to have a space where
this won't be an issue.

▶ An offering space—A section or space where your offerings go. If you are offering food on a regular basis, this might be a plate; if you are offering drink, then a cup. It can be a bowl for flowers. It should be placed before any depictions of your ancestors and idols (photos, statues, etc.) so it is clear who the offering is meant for.

➤ your tools–Your candles, jars, herbs and roots, oils, and everything else that you need should be at hand and stored here. You shouldn't need to regularly hunt through your home for what you need to work with.

MOVEABLE
ALTAR SPACES

I t's important to note that
this is "moveable" rather
than "temporary," because this
is not a temporary altar. You
may need to have a moveable
altar because you are not in a
stable living situation or the
people you live with do not

respect your practice, but that doesn't mean your altar isn't still a consistent part of your life. Your home may just be too small for a setup in a dedicated space. Whatever the reasons for needing a moveable altar, this is an option for anyone.

› container–

A space to hold everything, which might double as the surface as well! A milk crate where you can keep items or even an old suitcase that can be safely sealed and put away are great options. A serving tray that can

be picked up and moved easily
also works very well.

▸ **covering**–This follows
the same rules as for the
permanent space, but the
cloth itself will likely be much
smaller. Also, consider that this
cloth may need to be put on
the ground directly to create
an altar space to work at.

> **Work space**–Something
small and fireproof that you
can work upon and clean up
easily. A small baking sheet is
perfect. It will also double as
your offering space.

> **Your tools**–Since a
moveable altar will likely
be of a smaller size than a
permanent one, what you

are able to carry will not be as extensive—so it's best to stick to essential components. Everything you need should be stored in tightly sealed containers for safety.

Some general things you may have on your altar can include:

➤ Photos of ancestors
➤ Candles and candleholders

- Idols or their imagery
- Crystals
- Feathers
- Incense and incense burners

WHAT DO YOU NEED FOR HOODOO?

⊙—❖—⊙

THE TOOLS FOR HOODOO ARE VERY simple by necessity. They were developed and cultivated by people who historically did not have access to much more than what was in the home and what grew from the ground.

There are books, such as *Hoodoo Herb and Root Magic* by Catherine Yronwode, that provide information on plants, herbs, roots, and other items that can be used in a variety of works, but you don't need many things to start.

You will need some herbs and plants, and the ones listed here can be found in most grocery stores or local shops. Fresh herbs are always better for use in works, but that is not always possible for everyone. Even dried herbs are suitable to work with, so get whatever you can find in your area. Here are some very basic items to start with for your Hoodoo practice.

> **Rosemary–** A versatile herb used for matters of protection and love. Can be used in mojo bags, baths, and other work.

> **Chamomile-** This brings luck, especially in financial matters, but can also be used in protective works.

➤ **Salt**–As with most practices, it's used for protection and cleansing. Plain old table salt is fine to use, and any salt at all is acceptable.

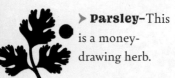

> **Parsley**–This is a money-drawing herb.

> **Olive oil**–Just the basic type that you can find in any grocery store. Hoodoo also incorporates a number of specialty oils, such as Van Van Oil, that are used for

many different works. Oil, in general, is used quite heavily as a component for a variety of works. Olive oil is a good, general purpose oil that can be used for just about anything.

▶ **Candles**–Candles come in many types, but basic, small, white candles are all you need at first. They're called *chime,* or emergency candles. If all you have are tea lights, those are fine (if a little small) to use as well.

Candles come in many different types and colors. Seven-day candles, the ones in large glass vessels that regularly have an image of a saint on them, are often used. For some work, specialty candles made in different forms like male and female figures, black cats, hearts, and skulls are used. But a white candle is all you need to get started.

❯ Jars and bottles–These are useful for both actual work and just to hold things. Herbs, oils, premade components, water, and so on can be placed in jars or bottles. They can be upcycled from other products, such as sauce and jam jars. They do not have to be purchased new.

► Curios—This is a catch all term for a legion of things. As mentioned before, Hoodoo is sympathetic work—like attracts like, and many curios work on this principle. They can be stones, shells, money, feathers, animal parts, dried plants, etc.

➤ **Crystals**—Hagstones and lodestones are both used traditionally, but there's no reason why you can't branch out and incorporate stones that speak to you and your needs. Rose quartz, coral, obsidian, and so on can be used.

DIVINATION

There are many forms of divination. Cultures around the world have their own forms of and reasons for divination. Hoodoo is no different and utilizes divination in various parts of the practice. During the early days of Hoodoo, divination could be used to diagnose ailments, but modern practitioners are far from likely to engage in this (outside of, perhaps, predicting the sex of a fetus). Divination is used primarily to commune with the spirit world and to get an idea of what life has in store. By performing divination or having it done on your behalf,

greater insight can be gained
into your relationship with the
spirit and physical world.

INFORMAL DIVINATION

The most common form of divination is just observation. The world is always telling us things as we pass through it. Many of us already have some of the knowledge needed to understand it, as it can be passed down in the form of superstitions. Think: Finding a penny on the ground is good luck if you pick it up (but only if it's face up!). These beliefs are such a part of life that we don't even consciously think of them. Often, though, we know many of them, such as the idea that a black cat crossing your path or walking under a ladder is bad luck.

These common beliefs or superstitions may not seem like divination, but learning to see them will help you in your practice. As you pay attention to the subtle movements of the world around you, you'll start to notice small patterns in your own life that will inform how you move through and understand the world.

Another way to get in tune
with the world, both seen
and unseen, is through dream
interpretation. Again, even
without formal training, there
are many superstitions about
dreams. For example, a dream
of fish means someone's
pregnant or will be soon.

Even without specific signs,
we can understand the general

feelings of dreams. Are they at peace, anxious, or sad? Spend time with the things you saw in your dream once you wake in the morning. Keep a journal and write things down. You may not get lotto numbers from your dreams, but careful consideration of them might help you understand more of your life and what's coming to you. *Llewellyn's Complete Dictionary of Dreams* by Dr. Michael Lennox has an extensive list of meanings for sorting out different images in dreams.

FORMAL DIVINATION

When people say divination, they're usually talking about the more formal, structured types. You can use any type that you are comfortable with. Many people start with playing cards because they are cheap and easy to

come by. *A Deck of Spells* by
Charles Porterfield has lovely
interpretations of playing cards
that can help new readers decide
if the card says yes or no.

Another
popular option for
performing your
own divination
is reading wax.
This is usually

done after some sort of work with a candle. The melted wax and leftover candle are read to see how things will turn out. It's fairly straightforward in that you look for images in the melted wax, like seeing shapes in clouds. This is where your practice in learning how to see comes in handy—it's great practice for finding shapes and images. Reading wax is a good way to gauge if your own work will be successful.

PROFESSIONAL DIVINATION

There are other divination practices such as tarot, bone reading, palmistry, cowrie shell reading, and many more, but all these take time and dedicated effort to learn. To practice these arts correctly and accurately, the reader must spend a good deal of time learning their craft. They are not the type of practices someone can pick up and master quickly. If you are interested in them, though, by all means commit yourself to their study!

But if you are only interested in having a reading, it's best to hire a professional. In Hoodoo,

seeking out a professional to
give a reading or just better
understand what you've been
seeing and feeling in the world
around you or in your practice
is common.

THE WORK

◉ ⋮ ⋮ ◉

HONEY/
SWEET JAR

This is a simple work that will help new practitioners get used to some of the most basic principles of Hoodoo work. A honey or sweet jar is almost exactly what it sounds like. It is a jar filled with a sweetener, and its purpose is to bring "sweetness" to an aspect of your life. This can be in the form of self-love, your relationship, your home, your job, mental health, or whatever else you would like to bring more positive energy to.

The jar should be glass with a metal lid. Reusing a jelly or sauce jar is perfectly fine. Make sure it is cleaned first!

The sweetener can be honey or sugar. Even syrup is fine. The jar will be sealed once it is set completely. You don't want to use anything that will go bad, so something sweet like juice, sugar water, or tea will not work for this purpose as it will spoil. This work calls for a sweet product that is shelf stable.

The final pieces in building the jar are the curios and herbs you'll be putting into it. What you use is entirely personal, but you will want to put in items that will attract the type of good fortune you're hoping for. Here are some suggestions to get you started, but don't be constrained by them. Figure out what feels good to you— it's your work!

▸ **For self-love:** rosemary, a selfie, a heart playing card, a chunk of rose quartz.

▶ **For a romantic relation-ship:** roses, a printout of a Lover's tarot card, an orange calcite.

▶ **For home life:** keys, Monopoly houses, salt.

▶ **For career/business:** coins or paper money, something that represents the business itself, cinnamon.

> **For any purpose:** write out what you want and put it into the jar. This can be done on a piece of paper (using a brown paper bag is traditional), and it is called a *petition*.

These are just suggestions to help you think of the type of small pieces you can add to your jar. Remember this is an act of sympathetic magic, so think about what represents the values and goals you have. Like attracts like. There might be things that make sense and have meaning only to you, and that's fine. It's your jar, your practice.

This part of the process may take some time for you to collect and decide on. There is no rush. Do not start until you feel you have everything you want to include in the jar. It can be as many or as few items as you like.

In addition to your jar and the curios, you will need a chime (emergency) candle.

When you are ready, go to your altar space, which should already be set up. This is where the jar will ultimately live. Think about your target desire—what you hope to achieve with the jar. How would you like that sweetness to manifest in your life? Pour the honey or other sweetener into the jar. Remember that you're going to add things to the jar, so you will want to leave a little room.

Now add the items you chose as well as the petition

you wrote out. You may need
to press them down a bit so
that they are coated in the
honey or other sweet medium.
While completing this, keep
your thoughts on your desires.
When the jar is full, put the lid
back on top.

Once the jar is sealed, take
up the candle. A plain white
candle is fine for this work, but

you can also pick a color that
aligns with your purpose. Dress
this candle with a little bit of
oil, spreading it
from the center
of the candle in
both directions.
You can also
use some herbs,
but you don't
need to. If you

choose to, rub the herbs onto
the candle in the same manner
as the oil or roll the candle
in them.

Melt a little wax from a
second candle and pour a
small amount onto the lid of
your jar. Place the first candle
in this pool while the wax is
still hot and hold for a few
seconds as it cools. This will

keep the candle upright. Light the dressed candle with your intentions in mind. Honey and other sweeteners are very slow to move, so adding the heat helps "charge" them and make them move faster for you. Spend some time with the jar as the candle is burning.

If you can stay near it and the candle is secure, allow it

to burn down. However, if you cannot stay near and there's a chance the candle may fall or be disturbed, snuff it out by covering the flame.

Repeat the candle burning regularly, always thinking about your desires. In time, they will flourish.

CANDLE BURNING FOR PEACEFUL HOME AND MONEY DRAW

The tools for Hoodoo are simple, but they can be used for a variety of things. Here are two different works using a candle, oil, and a few herbs.

For both of these, you will need a chime candle and a small holder to keep it upright. Chime candles burn down in about an hour, making it possible to complete a full work in a single sitting. If you do not have a chime candle, you can use a tea light if that is more accessible.

A straight pin, a safety pin, or even a sewing needle is also necessary. This is to inscribe directly in the candle wax your desired outcome or target.

PEACEFUL HOME

A white chime candle is perfectly fine, but you can also use pink or light blue. Pink and light blue are colors associated with peacefulness and familial or friendly love. Though the use of colored candles can be helpful, especially in communicating your desires more strongly, it is not necessary.

Think about what it means for your home to be peaceful. Is there currently an issue coming from inside (discord between members) or outside (loud neighbors) that is making it not peaceful? Imagine what the perfect situation would be for you.

With that in mind, take
up the pin and write words
that match your desire on the
chime. You could inscribe
something like *joy*, *time*, or
quiet. Choose carefully because
of the limited space.

Dress your candle by
applying a bit of oil, rubbing
from the center outward
in both directions, while

you continue to think on your desires. Apply some chamomile to the candle either by gently rubbing or rolling it on. When this is done, place the candle in its holder.

Light the candle and let it burn down. Think about what you want for your home while the candle burns.

MONEY DRAW

The process for drawing money is almost exactly the same as for the peaceful home. The only differences between the two are that the chime in the money draw is green and the herb is parsley.

All the same steps are followed for the work, but

the focus is on business, your career, and maybe a little luck.

OTHER VARIATIONS

This is very simple candle work and can be altered for love, luck, or just getting out of a bad situation. The actions are the same as above, but the components change. There are more complex candle rituals that involve multiple

or figurine candles as well as
different herbs and prayers.
But from this simple base
you can perform a number of
works simply by making small
changes and adding different
petitions.

FINISHING
AND DISPOSAL

After you've completed the burn, it's a good idea to attempt to read the wax so you know what to expect from the work. Spend some time looking over what was left, and see what you can find in it. Look up the meanings of

the images you found to see
if the work leaned positive or
negative. At the same time,
don't discount the relevance
of the symbol to you and your
life, even outside of the work.

For example, you might see
a bat, which is generally a bad
omen. But if your work was
meant to get your neighbor who
is always wearing a T-shirt with

a bat on it to move away, that might be a sign that the work has found its intended target.

Sometimes there may not be any wax left over, and that's a good sign!

If there is wax to dispose of, gather it and bury it in your yard. It's fine to bury the remains of positive work near you. Although not discussed

in this text, if you have done
any negative work, dispose
of it away from your home
at a crossroads. Please be
mindful of your environment,
and dispose of your works in
environmentally friendly ways.

HOME PROTECTION
AND CLEANSING

Your home should be a safe space where you can relax and engage with your loved ones and yourself. But what if it isn't? Many people feel uncomfortable in their own space. This small ritual will help to cleanse as well as protect your home. This can be done for a full house or a single room.

You only need two things: salt and a broom.

To start, open your windows to allow air to flow in. Thank the spirits for bringing you clean air to help you rid your space of negativity.

Then, from the back of the home or room, begin to sweep the floor, thinking of banishing those negative feelings. Although it's helpful, you do not need to actually sweep the floor for cleaning—you can go through the motions of sweeping. Go room to room, always starting in the back and moving to the door. If multiple

stories need to be done, start at the top and work your way to the bottom.

Sweep all this energy out of your front door. If you are only renting a room, then sweep the energy out of your bedroom door. If it's an apartment, then sweep into the apartment hallway. You want the energy out of your space. When you are finished, sprinkle a little salt in all four corners of the rooms and shut the windows. Move through your home in reverse with the salt, ending where you started.

This is a very simple

but intensely useful work that
helps ground you inside
of your home as you claim
it as your space. When you
are at your altar next, offer
thanks to spirits that helped
you cleanse your home by
lighting a bit of incense.

PARTING WORDS

HOODOO IS A LIVING, PRACTICAL tradition that is so much more than what could be covered in this book. The explanations and works contained in these pages are meant only as a primer to get you started. There's so much more in this vibrant, beautiful tradition.